INTRODUCTION

In the early days of jazz, musicians learned to play this new music th..ve language. They listened to the music played, searched for the new notes on their instruments and gradually combined them with the rhythms that moved these simple blues melodies with the beat.

Creating or improvising jazz music with others satisfies a basic need for self-expression and artistic fulfillment. That prime element will always be essential to this truly American art form. Successful improvisation requires a basic knowledge of scales, harmonies, musical form and adequate performance skills.

Today, jazz opportunities are available in most school music programs around the country. It is imperative that we continue to research and develop methods and materials that will help young musicians all over the world **PLAY AND LEARN** jazz music. The new **JAZZ ANYONE . . . ?** series is dedicated to that goal.

Note to Flute players using this book:

Some exercises in this book go below the Flute range. When this occurs, play these exercises up one octave (*8va*).

CD Tracking Sheet   CD #1

1. Tuning Notes - B♭/Jazz Track #1
2. Jazz Track #2
3. Ear Training Track #1
4. Jazz Track #3
5. Jazz Track #4
6. Jazz Track #5
7. Jazz Track #6
8. Jazz Track #7
9. Ear Training Track #2
10. Jazz Track #8
11. Jazz Track #9
12. Jazz Track #10
13. Jazz Track #11
14. Jazz Track #12
15. Jazz Track #13
16. Ear Training Track #3
17. Jazz Track #14
18. Jazz Track #15
19. Jazz Track #16
20. Jazz Track #17
21. Jazz Track #18
22. Jazz Track #19
23. Ear Training Track #4
24. Jazz Track #20
25. Jazz Track #21
26. Jazz Track #22
27. Jazz Track #23
28. Jazz Track #24
29. Jazz Track #25
30. Jazz Track #26
31. Ear Training Track #5
32. Jazz Track #27
33. Jazz Track #28
34. Jazz Track #29
35. Jazz Track #30
36. Jazz Track #31
37. Ear Training #6
38. Jazz Track #32
39. Jazz Track #33
40. Jazz Track #34
41. Jazz Track #35
42. Jazz Track #36
43. Ear Training Track #7
44. Jazz Track #37
45. Jazz Track #38
46. Jazz Track #39

CD Tracking Sheet   CD #2

1. Jazz Track #40
2. Jazz Track #41
3. Jazz Track #42
4. Jazz Track #43
5. Ear Training Track #8
6. Jazz Track #44
7. Jazz Track #45
8. Jazz Track #46
9. Jazz Track #47
10. Jazz Track #48
11. Jazz Track #49
12. Ear Training Track #9
13. Jazz Track #50
14. Jazz Track #51
15. Jazz Track #52
16. Jazz Track #53
17. Jazz Track #54
18. Jazz Track #55
19. Jazz Track #56
20. Ear Training Track #10
21. Jazz Track #57
22. Jazz Track #58
23. Jazz Track #59
24. Jazz Track #60
25. Jazz Track #61
26. Ear Training Track #11
27. Jazz Track #62
28. Jazz Track #63
29. Jazz Track #64
30. Jazz Track #65
31. Jazz Track #66
32. Jazz Track #67
33. Jazz Track #68
34. Ear Training Track #12
35. Jazz Track #69
36. Jazz Track #70
37. Jazz Track Blues Extra #1
38. Jazz Track Blues Extra #2
39. Jazz Track Blues Extra #3
40. Jazz Track Blues Extra #4

CD Tracking Sheet   CD #3

1. Bass Tuning Notes
2. Guitar Tuning Notes
3. Piano "A"
4. Jazz Rhythm Start-up Track #1
5. Jazz Rhythm Track #1
6. Jazz Rhythm Start-up Track #2
7. Jazz Rhythm Track #2
8. Jazz Rhythm Start-up Track #3
9. Jazz Rhythm Track #3
10. Jazz Rhythm Start-up Track #4
11. Jazz Rhythm Track #4
12. Jazz Rhythm Track #5 Exercise 1-3
13. Jazz Rhythm Track #5 Exercise 4-6
14. Jazz Rhythm Track #6
15. Jazz Rhythm Track #7 Exercise 1-3
16. Jazz Rhythm Track #7 Exercise 4-6
17. Jazz Rhythm Track #8
18. Jazz Rhythm Track #9
19. Jazz Rhythm Track #10
20. Special Jazz Rhythm Track
21. Jazz Rhythm Track #11
22. Jazz Rhythm Track #12

TABLE OF CONTENTS

4

FOREWORD

If you are playing jazz music for the very first time or just polishing a few previously acquired concepts and skills, the new **JAZZ ANYONE . . . ? PLAY AND LEARN** series will help you play this wonderful music better and better every day. This new series is ideal for individual study or as a practical classroom method for the entire jazz band.

THE PLAY AND LEARN FORMAT

The **PLAY AND LEARN** text introduces important concepts and performance opportunities involving the basic fundamentals of developing jazz melodies, rhythms and styles, improvisation and ear training. New information is framed in each lesson for easy identification. Content areas include:

. . . an introduction to the B♭ blues scale, harmonies and form
. . . an introduction to the F and B♭ Dorian minor mode
. . . the gradual evolution of swing jazz and jazz rock rhythms
. . . performing and improvising jazz with correct jazz style
. . . forming and developing the jazz rhythm section
. . . an introduction to the PENTATONIC language of jazz

RECORDED JAZZ TRACKS

Seventy JAZZ TRACKS organize a recorded reference of essential **PLAY AND LEARN** written concepts that are sequenced and developed throughout the text. Special **JAZZ RHYTHM TRACKS** also make it possible for beginning rhythm section players to hear and learn fundamentals quickly.

JAZZ VOCABULARY

New **JAZZ LICKS** or vocabulary is gradually introduced in each lesson and developed through repetition, exploration, ear training and application. Opportunities to improvise with the cassette tape or rhythm section are also provided in each lesson.

PUTTING IT ALL TOGETHER

You can **PUT IT ALL TOGETHER** at the end of each lesson as you apply the new vocabulary introduced in each lesson. **ETUDES** and **MINI-CHARTS** may be played with the cassette tape or with the entire jazz ensemble, making it possible to immediately **PLAY AND LEARN** each new concept.

THE BOTTOM LINE

Every good jazz musician has **"PAID THEIR DUES"** when it comes to hard work and long hours of practice. Great improvisation is a result of knowledge, experience and familiarity with the jazz language as well as creativity. Remember, if you're not playing, **YOU'RE NOT LEARNING!**

6

UNIT I

BLUES FUNDAMENTALS

The very essence of jazz music is rooted in its many forms of the blues. Blues moods are happy, sad, slow or fast and its melodies and harmonies can be simple or complex. The blues is fundamental to jazz music. Like many other art forms in America, the blues has experienced its own evolution. Today, the blues is **WORLD MUSIC** and it represents the freedom so important to us all.

┌─BLUES MELODIES ─────────────────────────────

Traditional blues melodies are based on a special scale called the blues scale. The blues scale is a combination of two elements, a five note minor pentatonic scale and the lowered fifth scale step of the key. The result is a six note blues scale that is usually related to a major scale as shown below.

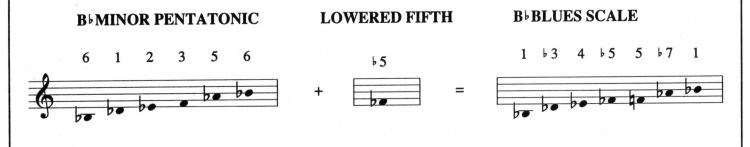

┌─BLUES HARMONIES ────────────────────────────

Three dominant seventh harmonies formed on the root (I), fourth (IV) and fifth (V) scale steps of a major scale are used in the traditional blues form. The roots (1) and sevenths (7) of each dominant chord are also found in the blues scale.

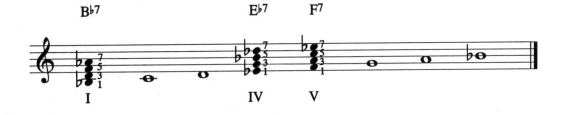

BLUES FORM

The following example shows the organization of these three dominant seventh chord harmonies (I7, IV7, V7) in the traditional twelve measure blues form. The blues is a three part song form. Part one is the **STATEMENT (A)**, part two is the **RESTATEMENT (A1)** and part three is the **ANSWER (B).**

(A) STATEMENT

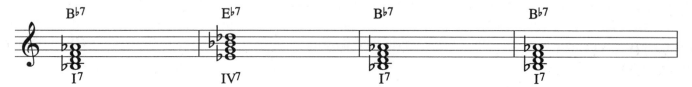

(A1) RESTATEMENT

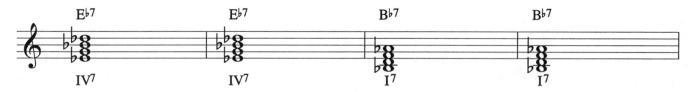

(B) ANSWER

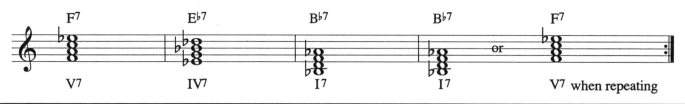

SYNCOPATING THE BEAT

Early musical training often teaches us to feel the down-beats or strong beats as the most important beats in the measure. In jazz rhythm, accents move the weak beats (pick-ups) to the strong beats across the bar line and within the measure to create an ongoing **SYNCOPATED BEAT LINE.**

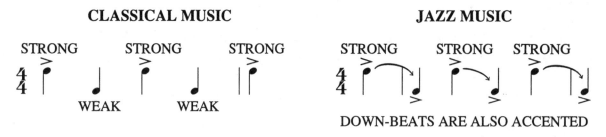

SWING STYLE JAZZ

Swing style jazz rhythms are not played the way they are written. In swing style, even eighth notes are played with a triplet feeling (12/8 meter) to create the swing eighth notes shown in the example below.

LESSON 1

JAZZ STYLE

Symbols are placed over the notes in jazz music to indicate how they are played. Four of these special markings have been identified below with a brief description of how each is played in the jazz style.

LEGATO NOTES (ƒ̄) should be started with a "D" attack and played smoothly with plenty of air. DO NOT SEPARATE legato notes from other notes. Think about the syllable DOO as you play legato notes.

BREATH ACCENTS (ƒ̇) should be started with a "D" attack and played as a SFORZANDO (sfz) with plenty of energy. Breath accented notes are NOT SEPARATED from other notes. Think about the syllable DOO or DAH as you play the breath accent.

HOUSE-TOP ACCENTS (ƒ̂) are played shorter than a breath accent but longer than a staccato. House-top accents are started with a "D" attack, ended with the tongue, and played with real energy! Think about the syllable DOOT when you play a house-top accent.

STACCATO NOTES (ƒ̇) are played as short as possible. They are started with a "D" attack and ended with the tongue. Think about the syllable DIT when you play staccato notes.

JAZZ TRACK #1 PLAYING THE BLUES

After you read the special information on style, let's **PLAY AND LEARN** some simple blues vocabulary. After you hear each pattern played by the horns, imitate the pattern in the open measures that follow. Try to play each vocabulary pattern exactly the way it is played.

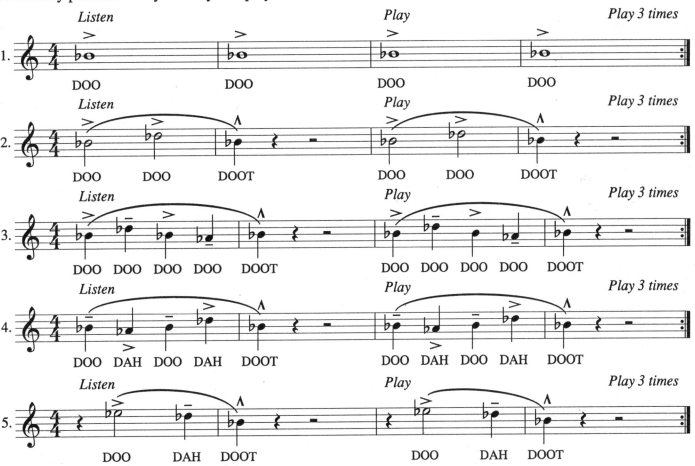

JAZZ TRACK #2 STARTING IMPROVISATION

Use the blues scale now to start making or improvising your own blues vocabulary. We will start by playing up and down the blues scale using quarter notes. Then in the second blues chorus, play up and down the blues scale changing directions as you combine quarter notes with half notes. Next, play shorter patterns with pick-up notes and finally, improvise melodies with larger intervals between some of the notes. Listen to the examples in the first few measures of each blues chorus, then, continue on with your own improvisation.

*Flute players reminder: play these exercises *8va*.

PLAYING WHAT YOU HEAR

Your mind must make a lot of simultaneous decisions to play what you have heard on your instrument. Developing this faculty through EAR TRAINING represents an important part of the improvisational process. Ask yourself the following questions if you have problems imitating unwritten patterns played on the cassette tape.

. . . how high or low is the starting note?
. . . where does the melody change direction?
. . . what is the highest or lowest melody note?
. . . on what beat does the melody start?
. . . what notes are on or off the beat?
. . . where are the rests?
. . . how long is the pattern?
. . . what are the dynamics?
. . . how did the pattern FEEL?

EAR TRAINING TRACK #1

Try to imitate the blues pattern you hear played in the space immediately following each pattern.

PUTTING IT ALL TOGETHER

This special section is included at the end of each lesson to give you an opportunity to put the concepts from each lesson into action. **Jazz Etude #1,** like those that follow, is composed with rhythms and melodies introduced in each lesson. If you are not playing these with your band, each ETUDE is recorded for you to hear and play. ETUDES are recorded once through with an open chorus immediately following that allows you to repeat the ETUDE by yourself with just the recorded accompaniment.

JAZZ TRACK # 3 JAZZ ETUDE #1

THE PLAY AND LEARN MINI-CHART

A simple four-part arrangement is written and recorded to help students develop the lesson concept in a large or small band setting. If you're not playing with the band, select one of the parts to play with the recording. Open choruses are provided for improvisation after each arrangement. Several riffs are suggested at the bottom of the page to play behind the soloist when you are playing with the band or with friends. After the improvisation, each **MINI-CHART** arrangement is played again with a special ending.

JAZZ TRACK # 4 "BLUES TIME"

LESSON 2

SWINGING JAZZ EIGHTH NOTES

When you play JAZZ MUSIC with others, it is important to know how traditional swing eighth note patterns are played. Articulation is fundamental in playing swing eighth notes. Thinking about syllables will help you articulate swing jazz eighth note patterns correctly.

1.( ) Many jazz patterns end with a syncopated off-beat eighth note. Start the first eighth note with a "D" attack and pop the final eighth note with a "T." DO NOT SEPARATE THE PAIR OF EIGHTH NOTES. Think, DOO-DIT, not TA-TAT.

2.( ) When a series of eighth notes occurs, play them smoothly from beat to beat. Start these patterns with a "D" attack and keep the air moving when you use the tongue! Think about the syllables DOO-N-DOO-DIT.

3.( ) When quarter notes are mixed with eighth notes, DO NOT RUSH eighth note patterns that proceed or follow. Let the accents help you move the pattern smoothly. Think about the syllables DOO-DOO-N-DOO-DIT.

4.( ) Longer eighth note patterns with pick-up notes may need special attention. CONCENTRATE ON THE BEAT as you play these patterns. Play the house-top accents in this pattern with a real punch and DO NOT SEPARATE THE EIGHTH NOTES THAT FOLLOW. Think about DOOT-DOOT-DOO-N-DOO-N-DOO-N-DOO-DIT. It never goes TA-TA-TA-TAT!

JAZZ TRACK #5 SWINGING THE BLUES

Listen carefully as you imitate these jazz patterns with eighth notes. Remember, use a legato attack and do not separate the eighth notes. Don't rush the eighth notes! Try to swing them evenly from beat to beat.

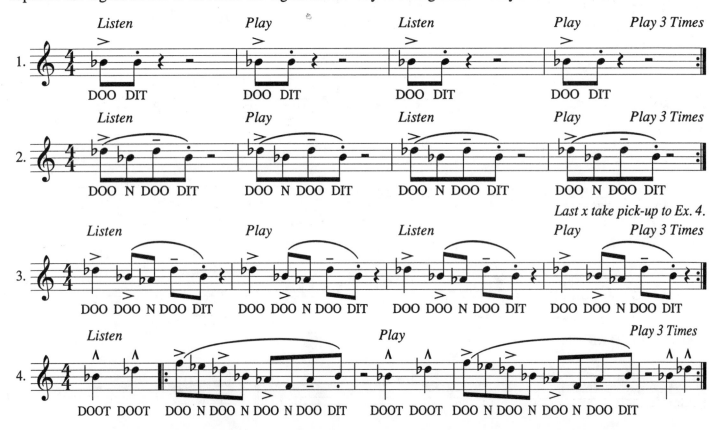

JAZZ TRACK #6 EXTENDING THE JAZZ EXPERIENCE

The blues patterns you have just played are combined now into an interesting jazz chorus. Play these patterns with the horns, then continue rearranging these same patterns in different ways in the second recorded blues chorus. To do this successively, you must memorize each jazz vocabulary pattern.

NOTE: A jazz pattern started on beats one or three has a different rhythmic feeling than when it is played on beats two and four. Try the examples below and then create your own patterns starting in these two different ways.

JAZZ TRACK #7 DEVELOPING JAZZ VOCABULARY

Making up jazz melodies to fit rhythm patterns is a part of the process that goes on in your mind when you are improvising. In the following exercises, the rhythms in the first pattern are used to form new melodies. Make up your own melodies with these same rhythms after you play the examples written in the following exercises.

EAR TRAINING TRACK #2

Imitate the following jazz patterns that you hear played on the recorded reference. If you have a problem playing them correctly, refer to the list of suggestions in Lesson 1 for help.

JAZZ TRACK #8 DEVELOPING JAZZ TECHNIQUE

You must develop a great deal of control on your instrument in order to play what you hear with correct jazz style and feeling. The following exercises provide examples of how to TAKE THE SCALES APART when you are practicing. Play each of the following patterns now with the horns.

NOTE: The previous patterns are only a few possibilities for working systematically through the blues scale. Write your own patterns, then play them with the open choruses of blues on the cassette tape.

PUTTING IT ALL TOGETHER

The same format is used for each concluding session. ETUDES are recorded and followed by an open chorus of blues for students to use in repeating each ETUDE with just the rhythm section. The MINI-CHART format remains the same throughout the text. Each arrangement is recorded once through and is followed by an open chorus for repeating the etude or improvisation. Riffs for solo reinforcements are suggested at the bottom of the page.

JAZZ TRACK #9 JAZZ ETUDE #2

JAZZ TRACK #10 BLUESIN' ON

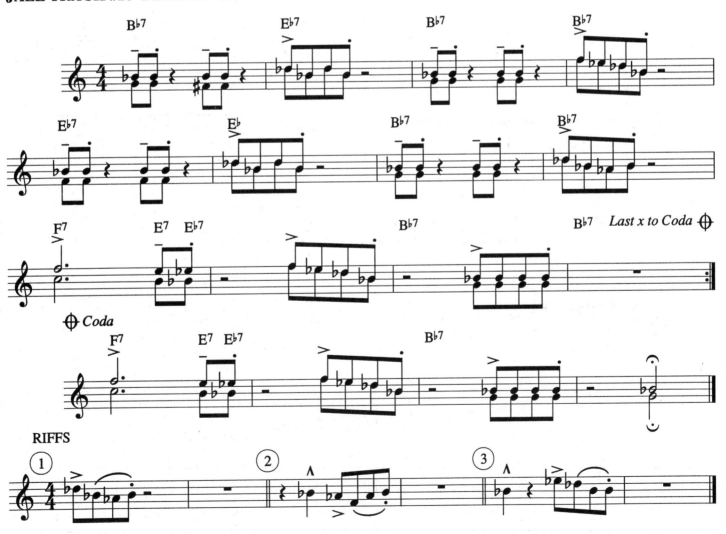

LESSON 3

JAZZ ROCK

The vitality of rock music is an important part of today's jazz idiom. Jazz rock music is usually associated with high-energy. However, jazz rock music is not always loud. It is important to develop experience with the jazz rock style. The following information will help you play jazz rock music correctly.

THINGS TO REMEMBER WHEN PLAYING JAZZ ROCK

1. ♩ ♩ ♩ ♩ Style markings are played the same in jazz rock music.

2. DOOS, DAHS, DOOTS & DITS These same syllables are used for the sounds of jazz rock special note styles.

3. ♪♪ ♪♪♪ Jazz rock eighth notes are played as written with a steady even feeling in 8/8 meter.

4. ♪♪♪♪ ♪♪ Concentrate on the accented up-beats and down-beats to keep longer eighth note jazz rock patterns from rushing.

5. ♩ ♩ Quarter notes in jazz rock music are often shown as a staccato under a house-top.

JAZZ TRACK #11 JAZZ ROCK BLUES

Imitate the jazz rock patterns formed with blues vocabulary patterns similar to those introduced in LESSON 2. Notice how different these patterns feel when they are played in the JAZZ ROCK style.

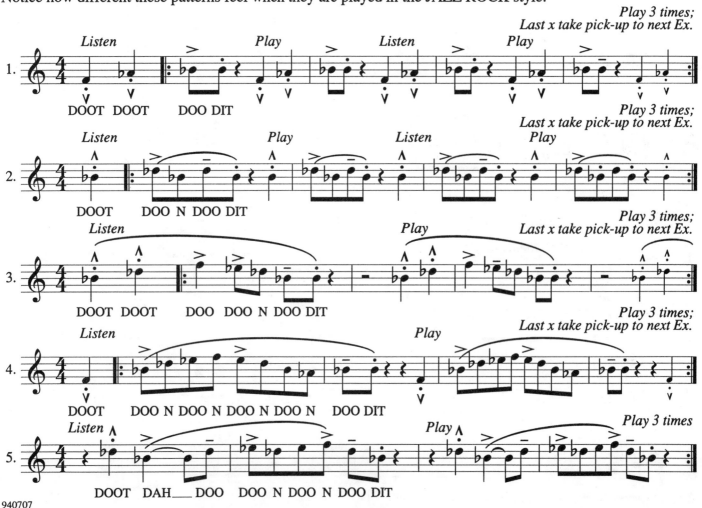

940707

JAZZ TRACK #12 EXTENDING THE JAZZ EXPERIENCE

Previous exercises are combined to form an interesting chorus of jazz rock blues. Play these now with the horns as they are written, then rearrange them as you wish in the second recorded chorus of rock blues.

JAZZ TRACK #13 DEVELOPING JAZZ ROCK IMPROVISATION

Use simple rhythm patterns as you begin processing the blues scale for improvisation. Eventually, combine these rhythms into longer patterns. Make up your own melodies with the rhythms played by the horns in each phrase of the following exercises. Suggested melodies are written in the open spaces of your text.

EAR TRAINING TRACK #3

Imitate the following jazz rock blues patterns now. Listen carefully to play them with correct jazz rock style.

PUTTING IT ALL TOGETHER

JAZZ TRACK #14 JAZZ ETUDE #3

JAZZ TRACK #15 ROCKIN' THE BLUES

LESSON 4

THE FLATTED FIFTH (♭5)

Tension and color are created in a blues melody when the lowered or flatted fifth (♭5) scale step is added. This important note should not always be used as a passing tone. This is an important reason for learning to pattern the blues scale with and without the flatted fifth. Many rhythm patterns will not work when the flatted fifth (♭5) is added.

JAZZ TRACK #16 PLAYING THE FLATTED FIFTH (♭5)

Imitate the examples of the flatted fifth after each is played now on the cassette tape. Notice how they are "scooped or bent" when they are played.

JAZZ TRACK #17 THE FLATTED FIFTH (♭5) IN ACTION

It is important not to separate a final syncopated eighth note that is tied into a longer note. It is also important not to rush these syncopated rhythms. Notice how the eighth notes are syncopated in Exercise 4 by accenting the off-beat eighth notes. Think about the correct syllables as you play each pattern.

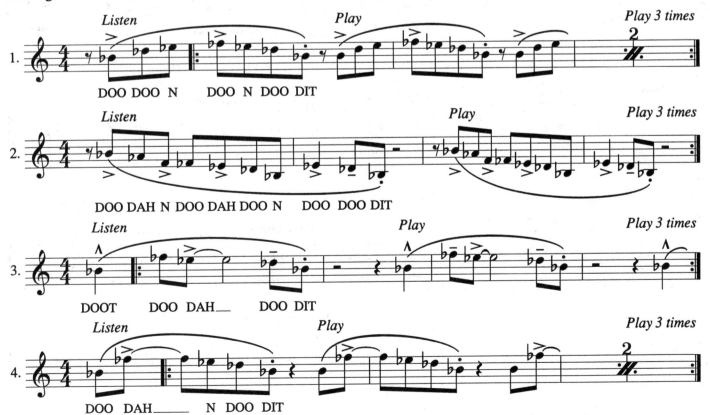

JAZZ TRACK #18 EXTENDING THE JAZZ EXPERIENCE

Previous patterns are combined again to create another typical blues chorus. Play these now with the horns, then reorganize the same patterns on your own in the second recorded chorus.

THE SIX NOTE BLUES SCALE WITH A ♭5

Practice improvising blues melodies with the extended six note blues scale. You will find that many rhythms are difficult to pattern when the flatted fifth (♭5) is added.

JAZZ TRACK #19 ACCENTING SYNCOPATED EIGHTH NOTES

Shifting to the off-beat eighth notes is a traditional way of creating greater rhythmic variety in jazz music. Imitate some familiar patterns now, with the accents placed on the syncopated eighth notes.

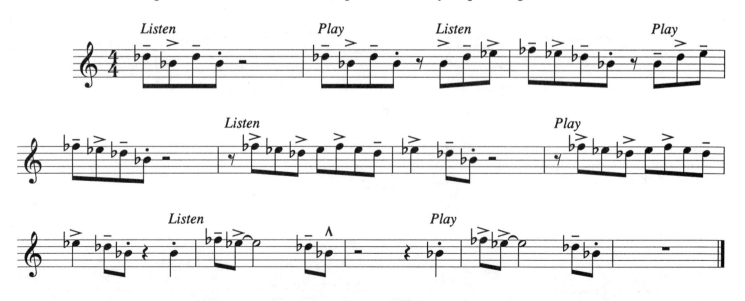

EAR TRAINING TRACK #4

Imitate the unwritten patterns now with the cassette tape. Try to identify the new flatted fifth sound as you play through these jazz patterns.

REPETITION AND MEMORIZATION

One of the best ways to memorize music is through repetition. Every exercise presented in this text should be played many times with and without the cassette tape reference. It is impossible to memorize and use jazz vocabulary for improvisation that you cannot play. Reliable and usable musical memorization usually results from hours of conscientious practice developing good instrumental technique.

JAZZ TRACK #20 DEVELOPING JAZZ TECHNIQUE

Processing a rhythm pattern through the blues scale will improve your instrumental technique and improvisational skills. Two simple rhythms are used now to demonstrate this important concept. Imitate these now in the space following each pattern.

PUTTING IT ALL TOGETHER

JAZZ TRACK #21 JAZZ ETUDE #4

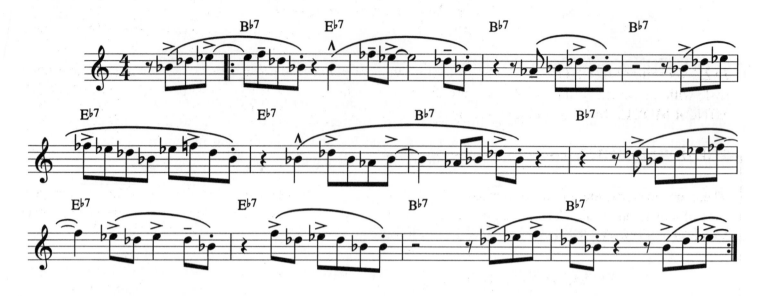

JAZZ TRACK #22 BLUEDODIT

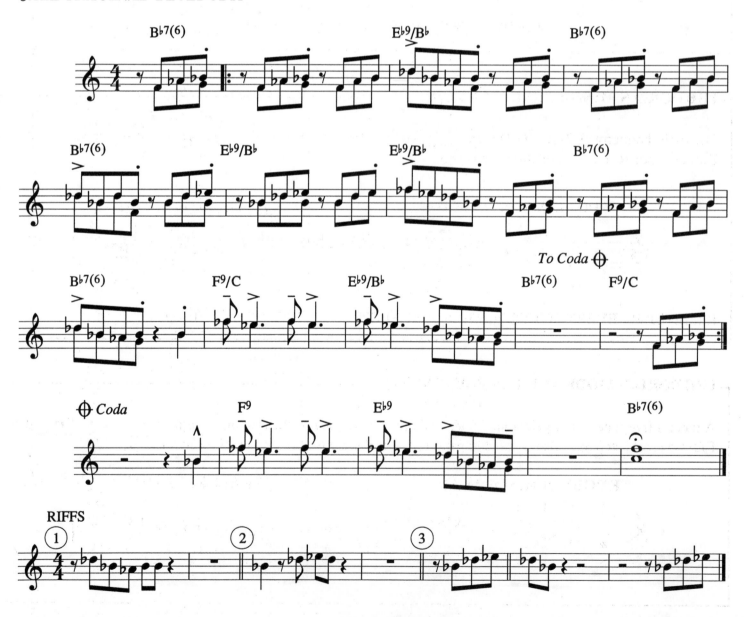

UNIT II

IN A MINOR MODE

JAZZ vocabulary in **UNIT I** is formed from the five note minor pentatonic blues scale and the six note blues scale with the flatted fifth (♭5). We will use these same scales in **UNIT II** to form vocabulary for the **DORIAN MINOR MODE.** Most minor harmonies in jazz music (II-7) are based on the Dorian scale.

THE DORIAN MODE

There are seven different notes or pitches in each major scale. Each note of a major scale can be the fundamental tone of a different mode. The Dorian scale is called a second degree scale or a scale starting on the second scale step of a major scale. The example below shows this relationship.

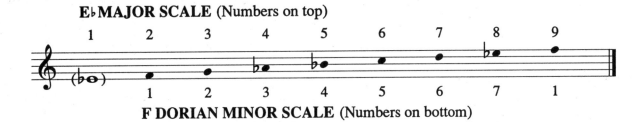

THE DORIAN MINOR TONIC I-7 CHORD

The tonic harmony (I-7) of the Dorian mode is formed on the root, third, fifth and seventh scale steps of the Dorian minor scale. This relationship is shown below.

REMEMBER: EVERY OTHER NOTE OF A SCALE IS USED TO FORM A CHORD.

THE DORIAN MODE AND THE BLUES SCALE

A natural five note minor pentatonic blues scale may be formed on the root of a Dorian minor scale. The flatted fifth (♭5) scale step may also be used in patterning vocabulary for the Dorian minor harmonies.

LESSON 5

JAZZ TRACK #23 EXPLORING THE DORIAN MINOR HARMONY

After reading and studying the special information presented in the **UNIT II** overview, listen to the blues scale as it is played with a minor harmony formed on the root of a Dorian minor scale. Play up and down this scale as the minor harmony continues to sound on the cassette tape. Occasionally add the flatted fifth (♭5) scale step.

F DORIAN MINOR BLUES SCALE

JAZZ TRACK #24 DORIAN MINOR VOCABULARY

Imitate the one measure patterns as you have in previous lessons. Notice that these patterns are similar to those previously used in the blues. We will use an eight (8) measure form.

JAZZ TRACK #25 TWO MEASURE MINOR PATTERNS

Imitate these two measure patterns with the new Dorian minor harmonies. We will continue to use the eight (8) measure form.

JAZZ TRACK #26 EXTENDING THE JAZZ EXPERIENCE

Imitating and memorizing longer vocabulary patterns plays an important role in developing a stronger sense of phrasing. Listen carefully to each pattern. As you imitate these patterns, try not to look at the music.

┌─IMPROVISING IN THE DORIAN MODE────────────────────────────

I am sure that you have noticed that we are no longer playing the twelve measure blues form. We are now playing **EIGHT MEASURE PHRASES** and no longer have the changing harmonies to assist us in keeping our place. This is an important consideration when improvising songs with extended minor harmonies. Use the following example of up- and down-beat phrases to help you feel a natural **FOUR MEASURE PHRASE.**

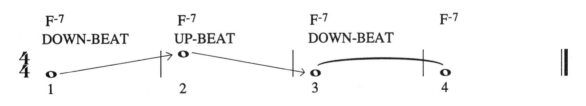

EAR TRAINING TRACK #5

Imitate each pattern formed with the new Dorian minor scale after it is played on the cassette tape.

PUTTING IT ALL TOGETHER

JAZZ TRACK #27 JAZZ ETUDE #5

JAZZ TRACK #28 A TOUCH OF MINOR

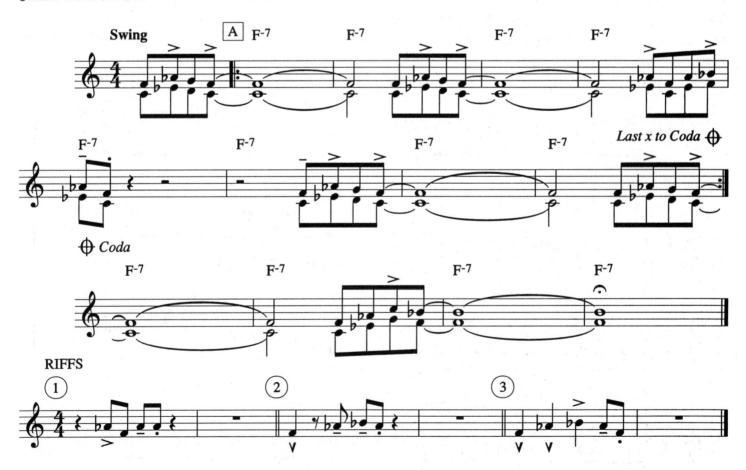

LESSON 6

MORE DORIAN MINOR

It is always helpful to apply the jazz vocabulary we learn in one key to other keys. Even though we are playing in the same key as **UNIT I,** you will find that with a minor harmony, the same scale sounds and feels different. The blues scale can be played with greater freedom when the basic harmony is minor and doesn't change.

A♭ MAJOR SCALE (Numbers on top)

B♭ DORIAN SCALE (Numbers on bottom)

B♭ BLUES SCALE   CHORD SYMBOL B♭-7/B♭m7/I-7

JAZZ TRACK #29 FORMING SIMPLE MINOR VOCABULARY

After carefully reading and studying the information above, form some basic jazz vocabulary now for the Dorian minor harmony. Imitate these patterns now as you have in previous lessons.

JAZZ TRACK #30 DEVELOPING THE MINOR PATTERNS

Imitate these two measure phrases now with the Dorian minor harmonies. Notice how the larger skips create different sounding melodies.

JAZZ TRACK #31 EXTENDING THE JAZZ EXPERIENCE

Continue forming longer phrases with each new scale. Remember, rhythm creates the action in music. Plan your rhythms and work them through the scales. Space is important.

EAR-TRAINING TRACK #6

Imitate the patterns now with the cassette tape. Notice how these patterns sound different in a minor key.

PUTTING IT ALL TOGETHER

JAZZ TRACK #32 JAZZ ETUDE #6

JAZZ TRACK #33 MINOR A LA MODE (Jazz Rock)

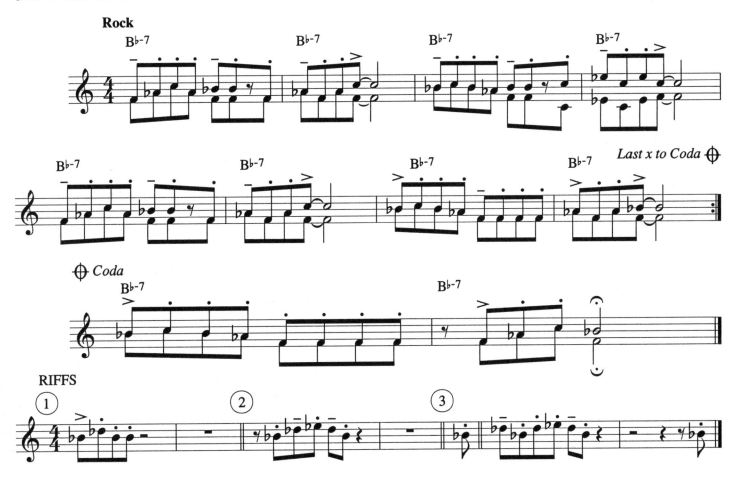

LESSON 7

PLAYING IN DIFFERENT KEYS

Learning to play jazz patterns in different keys is an important step in expanding your jazz vocabulary. Notice the similarities between the two minor blues scales previously introduced.

F MINOR PENTATONIC SCALE **F BLUES SCALE**

Bb MINOR PENTATONIC SCALE **Bb BLUES SCALE**

JAZZ TRACK #34 MOVING JAZZ VOCABULARY PATTERNS

Playing the same jazz pattern in different keys is a good way to develop new vocabulary. We will do this now with the simple patterns below.

JAZZ TRACK #35 MOVING LONGER JAZZ PATTERNS

Imitate these longer patterns now in two different keys. Play these patterns until you can play them in both keys from memory.

JAZZ TRACK #36 EXTENDING THE JAZZ EXPERIENCE

In the following exercises, two-measure patterns are written and played for you to imitate in the second key without music. Writing these patterns will help you find them.

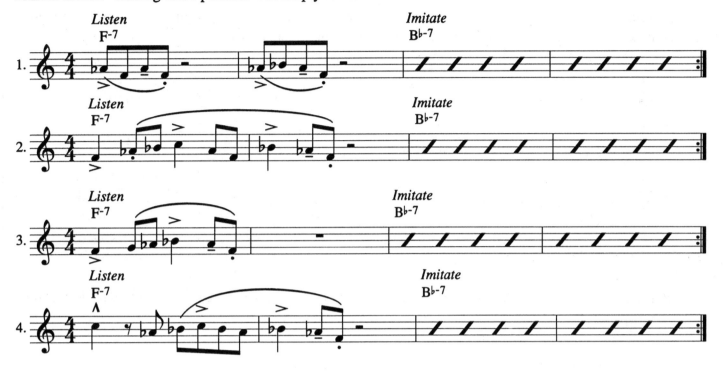

EAR-TRAINING TRACK #7

Listen carefully as you imitate the following patterns in two different keys.

JAZZ TRACK #37 KEEPING YOUR PLACE

The following eight-measure phrase is a mini-ABA song form. Use the up- and down-beat phrase concept to help you keep your place in the form as you improvise with the changing harmonies.

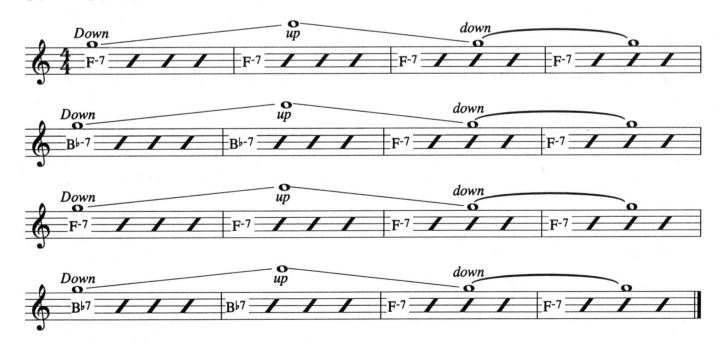

32

PUTTING IT ALL TOGETHER

JAZZ TRACK #38 JAZZ ETUDE #7

JAZZ TRACK #39 A MINOR CHANGE

940707

LESSON 8

┌─**ADDING NEW NOTES** ─────────────────────────────────

Creating melodic and harmonic tension is important in all styles of music. It is possible to create this tension in the Dorian minor mode. Simply add the second scale step of the Dorian scale to the minor pentatonic scale formed on its root. When this note is added at the top of the scale it is called the ninth and a 9 replaces the 7 beside the chord name to indicate the addition of the ninth to the chord.

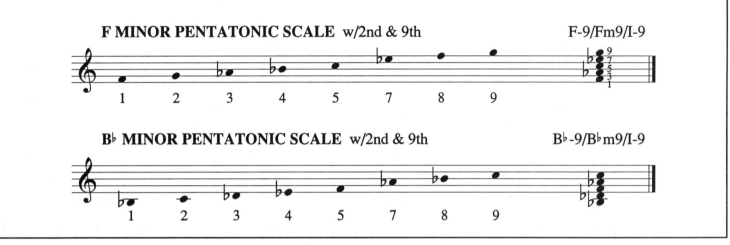

JAZZ TRACK #40 EXPLORING THE NEW SOUND

After carefully reading and studying the information above, listen for the new notes that are added in the recorded example with each minor chord. Try these new sounds with the piano as it continues to play the Dorian minor tonic chord after each example.

JAZZ TRACK #41

Play these patterns now, listening very carefully for the new notes that are added to both Dorian minor scales.

JAZZ TRACK #42 PLAYING THE DORIAN SCALE

It is important to begin using the entire Dorian scale when you are improvising. Imitate these full Dorian minor scale patterns now with the cassette tape.

JAZZ TRACK #43 BROKEN SCALE PATTERNS

Playing broken scale patterns up and down the scale is another way to add variety to your blues vocabulary. Try these patterns now with the cassette tape.

EAR-TRAINING TRACK #8

Longer patterns using the complete Dorian scale are recorded for your ear training. Listen carefully to determine the correct key.

PUTTING IT ALL TOGETHER

JAZZ TRACK #44 JAZZ ETUDE #8

Medium rock

JAZZ TRACK #45 MINOR YOURS?

Bossa rock

*RIFFS

*NOTE: To be played during first 8 measures only!

UNIT III

MORE BLUES

As important as rhythms are, it is still necessary to hear the melodies you are forming with the rhythms. The blues provides an excellent basis for developing this technique. By now, you should be familiar enough with the sound of the blues scale to use it fluently in composing blues melodies with the more difficult triplet rhythms introduced in UNIT III.

RHYTHM AND BLUES

The ability to quickly compose jazz melodies to fit jazz rhythms is the essence of jazz improvisation. In previous lessons, this concept is reinforced with numerous exercises. The more you practice processing melodies with rhythms the easier it becomes. One of the secrets to better improvisation lies in the continuous learning and development of new and more complicated rhythms and scales.

SYNCOPATED RHYTHMS

We have already been introduced to syncopation with eighth note pick-ups and final eighth note syncopation introduced in UNIT I and UNIT II. In UNIT III, we will learn to play longer syncopated swing jazz rhythms that anticipate the beat. This concept is called TRIPLETIZING. The rhythm pattern is turned into a series of triplets with the main rhythms accented as the triplets are played.

The following rhythms introduced in LESSON 9 are outlined below with a brief explanation about the beats they anticipate. These are some of the most difficult jazz rhythms to master. Think about the jazz syllables when you play each pattern.

DOOT DOOT DOO DIT DOOT

This rhythm anticipates the third and fourth beats.

DOO DIT DOO DAH

This rhythm anticipates the second beat and the down-beat of the next measure.

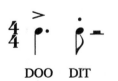
DOO   DIT

This rhythm anticipates the third beat.

DOO— DIT DOO DIT

This rhythm anticipates the down-beat.

LESSON 9

JAZZ TRACK #46 SYNCOPATING SWING JAZZ TRIPLETS

Playing accented eighth note swing triplets on each beat of the measure will help you develop the articulation and finger technique necessary in playing triplets evenly. Accent the first note of the triplet group now as you play through a chorus of swing style blues on the root of the blues scale.

Next, syncopate these swing jazz eighth note triplets by accenting the last eighth note in each triplet group. Play these syncopated triplets now with the next chorus of blues. Make sure the triplets are played evenly with a steady beat.

JAZZ TRACK #47 TRIPLETIZING SWING JAZZ RHYTHMS

In the following exercises triplets are added between the notes of the new rhythms of the **"PLAY"** section. The horns will play these TRIPLETIZED patterns for you to answer now. Each pattern should be played as written in the final measures of each exercise.

1.

2.

3.
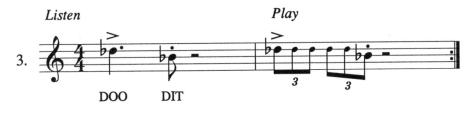

4.

JAZZ TRACK #48 EMPHASIZING CHORD TONES

Leading your melody to the roots of the harmonies creates a strong and effective vocabulary pattern. It takes practice and control to accomplish this consistently. Play examples of this technique now with the cassette tape. Try this on your own in the second chorus of open blues.

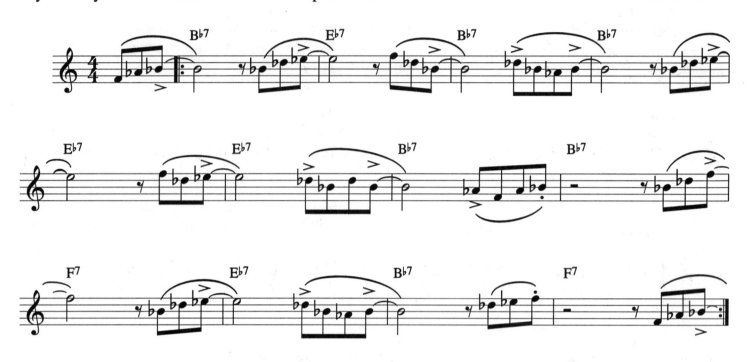

JAZZ TRACK #49 MORE PATTERNS ON CHORDAL TONES

Thinking about the moving harmonies as you create melodies is the beginning of playing through the chord changes. Playing patterns formed on the roots of the chords is a good way to start this process. Notice how short and precise the patterns are as you play them now with the horns. Try creating some of your own in the second chorus of recorded blues.

EAR TRAINING TRACK #9 Imitate the swing jazz patterns now with the cassette tape.

JAZZ TRACK #50 SYNCOPATED JAZZ ROCK

Play the exercise patterns from LESSON 9 in a sixteen-measure jazz rock format. Notice how the articulation changes in the jazz rock style as you imitate these minor patterns

JAZZ TRACK #51 MORE DORIAN MINOR JAZZ SWING

Use the following patterns as an example in creating your own jazz melodies using the notes of the minor harmony. Notice how each pattern outlines a part of the minor ninth chord.

PUTTING IT ALL TOGETHER

JAZZ TRACK #52 JAZZ ETUDE #9

JAZZ TRACK #53 MORE BLUES

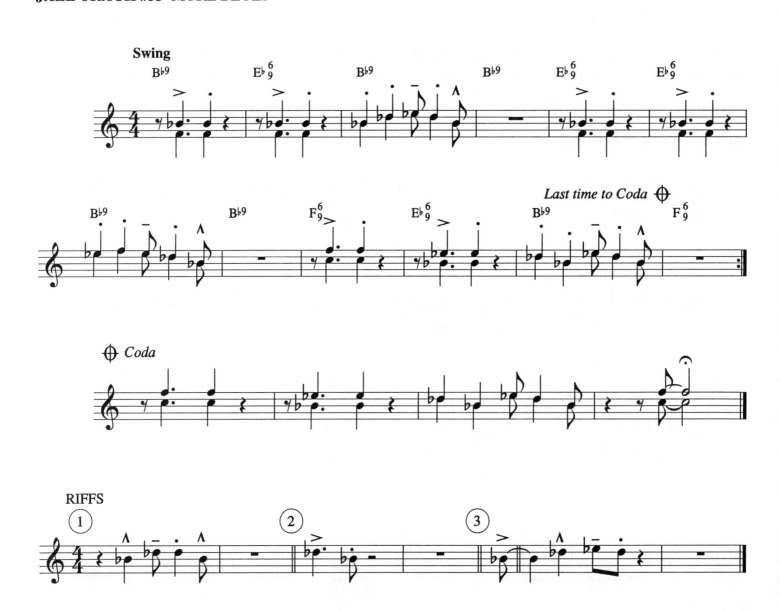

LESSON 10

EIGHTH NOTE TRIPLETS

Practicing extended eighth note triplet patterns will help you develop the stamina and control needed for smooth and even playing. It takes a great deal of practice before eighth note triplets can be used fluently for improvisation. Consider the following information before you play the exercises in LESSON 10.

1. Eighth note triplets start jazz melodies with energy.

2. Eight note triplets add momentum to a jazz melody.

3. Adding eighth note triplets to regular eighth notes moves the melody.

4. Eighth note triplets extend and develop melody patterns.

5. Eighth note triplets may be slurred or lightly tongued.

6. Keep the air moving when playing eighth notes on wind instruments.

JAZZ TRACK #54 THE TRIPLET BLUES

The following exercises will help you develop facility with eighth note triplet patterns. If you have problems with these patterns, practice them slowly with your metronome. Make sure you listen carefully to each example, especially the accents. Don't let the triplets lag behind. Play them with energy and move them evenly from beat to beat.

JAZZ TRACK #55 EXTENDING THE JAZZ EXPERIENCE

Continue combining the exercises from each lesson into a variety of blues choruses. These triplet patterns are not as easy to combine as the less complex eighth note patterns. Notice how the same patterns change their rhythmic feel when they are started on the strong or weak beats of the measure.

JAZZ TRACK #56 TRIPLET TECHNIQUE

Breaking the blues scale into two and three note triplet patterns will build flexibility and finger coordination. Slur or lightly tongue these patterns, making certain that each note is clear and that each triplet group is played evenly from beat to beat.

EAR TRAINING TRACK #10 Imitate these unwritten triplet patterns now.

PUTTING IT ALL TOGETHER

JAZZ TRACK #57 JAZZ ETUDE #10

JAZZ TRACK #58 BLUES OUT!

LESSON 11

SYNCOPATED TRIPLETS

Syncopated triplet eighth notes create exciting rhythms in jazz music. Improvising fluently with these rhythms requires a great deal of instrumental coordination and flexibility. Read the following information before you play the lesson.

1. Syncopated eighth note triplets anticipate the beat.

2. The final note of a triplet group syncopates the beat.

3. Accenting different notes of a triplet group creates rhythmic variety.

4. Playing only the first two notes of the triplet group is effective.

5. Starting pick ups on the second note of a triplet group moves the melody.

6. Always accent a final eighth note triplet tied to another note.

JAZZ TRACK #59 BLUES AND SYNCOPATED TRIPLETS

The following patterns introduce a variety of syncopated triplet rhythms. If you have problems playing any of these patterns, work them out slowly with your metronome. Make sure every note is played with precision.

JAZZ TRACK #60 EXTENDING THE JAZZ EXPERIENCE

Combine and develop syncopated rhythms as you have in previous lessons. Play these combined rhythms for
LESSON 11 then rearrange the same rhythms in the open blues chorus that follows.

JAZZ TRACK #61 SYNCOPATED TRIPLET MELODIES

Process LESSON 11 syncopated triplet rhythms now with a variety of blues scale melodies. Play the following
examples with the horns, then continue creating different melodies with the same rhythms.

EAR TRAINING TRACK #11 Imitate these unwritten syncopated patterns now.

PUTTING IT ALL TOGETHER

JAZZ TRACK #62 JAZZ ETUDE #11

JAZZ TRACK #63 BABY BLUES

RIFFS

LESSON 12

IMPORTANT JAZZ RHYTHMS

The following rhythms create a strong feeling of syncopation by anticipating several beats in a row. Long or short notes may be used for these extended anticipations. This rhythmic technique is very effective when played correctly. Read the information below before you play the exercise in LESSON 12.

1. Play these eighth notes with a real snap. Don't let them fall on the beat! Use the DIT syllable for these short eighth notes.

2. This rhythm pushes your melody forward with energy. Don't let it lag behind the beat. Use a DOO attack and push each long breath accent with plenty of air.

3. Quarter note triplets are usually played with breath accents. This polyrhythm distributes three pulses evenly over two beats. Start these long breath accents with a strong DOO attack and plenty of air.

4. Combining a series of syncopated notes with other rhythms is always an effective way to create interesting rhythm patterns. Playing mixed rhythm patterns correctly takes concentration and practice. Syncopated notes in a series may be played long or short. Use a DOO or DAH for long notes and a DIT or DOOT for the short notes.

SYNCOPATING THE BLUES

Use the 12/8 triplet feeling to help you play syncopated notes in a series with correct jazz style.

JAZZ TRACK #64 SYNCOPATING THE BLUES

Read and study carefully the information given above before playing the following exercises. Placing these extended syncopated eighth notes correctly depends on the accuracy of your triplet concept. If necessary, TRIPLETIZE these rhythms as you imitate them now.

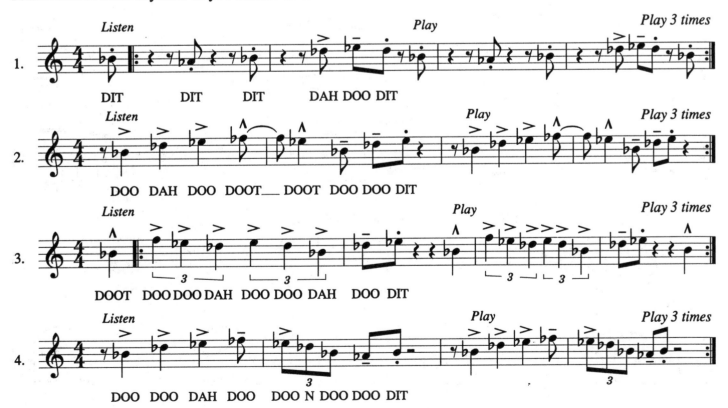

JAZZ TRACK #65 EXTENDING THE JAZZ EXPERIENCE

Memorize and combine the extended syncopated patterns from LESSON 12 as you have done in previous lessons. Play the examples below now and then create your own combinations in the open blues chorus that follows. Don't forget to start these patterns on different beats of the measure.

JAZZ TRACK #66 COMBINING SYNCOPATED RHYTHMS

The following patterns tie the different syncopated rhythms together into longer four measure phrases. Listen to the patterns played correctly, then imitate each pattern twice in the final eight measures of the open blues chorus that follow. Listen to the phrase played in the first 4 measures of the blues, then imitate them in the final 4 measures.

JAZZ TRACK #67 MINOR MODE JAZZ SWING

We will play the same jazz rhythms now in eight measure phrases using the Dorian minor harmony. This exercise will be played in the swing style.

JAZZ TRACK #68 LONGER MINOR SWING JAZZ MELODIES

The Dorian blues scale is used in forming the following patterns. Listen to each of the longer patterns, then imitate it with the space provided with the rhythm section. You may have to listen to these patterns several times to imitate them correctly.

EAR TRAINING TRACK #12 Imitate the blues patterns with the cassette tape.

PUTTING IT ALL TOGETHER

JAZZ TRACK #69 JAZZ ETUDE #12

JAZZ TRACK # 70 RAD ROCK BLUES

UNIT IV

SOME BLUES EXTRAS

The following **BLUES EXTRAS** provide experience with blues in other common keys. By now, you will no doubt be able to play most rhythm patterns correctly in the keys we have studied. So, it will be easy for you to **PLAY AND LEARN** the materials presented now in several new keys of **UNIT IV**.

WORKING THROUGH THE BLUES EXTRAS

The BLUES EXTRAS format introduces the blues scale for each new key, simple to more complex rhythm patterns and a harmonized chorus of blues in the new key to use in making up backgrounds for the **ETUDES** or improvisation. Three **JAZZ ETUDES** are written to help you develop facility in each new key.

THINGS TO DO

When using **PLAY AND LEARN** with the entire band, the blues form harmonies that can be converted into a variety of interesting rhythm backgrounds to play behind the **ETUDES** or soloists. The full harmonies can be played by either the saxophones or the brass, making it possible for one of the sections to play the background while the other section plays the **ETUDE**. These harmonies may also be used to help tune your sections. Memorizing your part allows you to use it freely in a variety of **PLAY AND LEARN** jazz experiences.

WRITING JAZZ MUSIC

Today, in the professional world of music, many jazz musicians make their living writing jazz music. Composing simple blues melodies, putting them with rhythms and writing them down is how it often starts. Learning to write what you hear will soon lead you to wanting to hear what you write. Learning to create and write good jazz melodies is an excellent beginning in learning to compose and arrange music. With a little help from your teacher, it's not impossible to begin harmonizing and transposing the things you write for all of the instruments to play. Try it, you'll like it!

JAZZ TRACKS FOR BLUES EXTRAS

Each **ETUDE** and two open blues are recorded by the rhythm section in each new key. Use the recordings to practice your **ETUDES** and for improvising in the new keys. An excellent way to monitor progress is to tape yourself playing with the **JAZZ TRACKS**. This allows you to **HEAR IT LIKE IT IS!**

JAZZ TRACK BLUES EXTRA #1

F BLUES SCALE

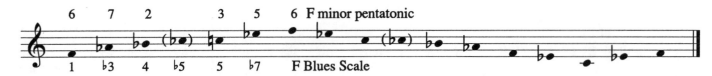

F BLUES JAZZ ETUDES

BLUES EXTRA #1 F BLUES

JAZZ TRACK BLUES EXTRA #2

C BLUES SCALE

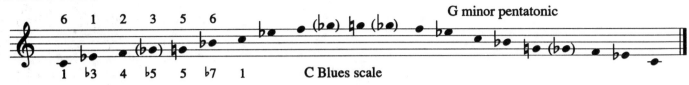

G minor pentatonic

C Blues scale

C BLUES JAZZ ETUDES

C BLUES HARMONIES

JAZZ TRACK BLUES EXTRA #3

G BLUES SCALE

G BLUES JAZZ ETUDES

G BLUES HARMONIES

JAZZ TRACK BLUES EXTRA #4

E♭ BLUES SCALE

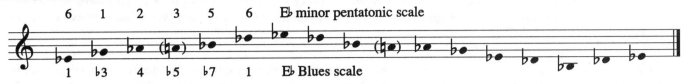

E♭ BLUES JAZZ ETUDES

E♭ BLUES HARMONIES

THE JAZZ ANYONE . . . ? STORY

JAZZ ANYONE . . . ? has been in process for many years. It started the day I picked up my trumpet and fell in love with music. Through my junior and high school band years, learning and performing with local pro bands, weekly jam sessions at several sites in my home town, Orlando, Florida, and a win on the national Horace Heidt Show, convinced me that music was my way.

I earned a Bachelor of Music degree at the University of Alabama where numerous influences inspired me and moved jazz into center focus. Little did I realize that someday I would be putting all of these experiences into a learning form of my own.

After college, the Third Army Band in Atlanta, Georgia, provided around-the-clock jazz opportunities which included jazz lessons from pianist, Wynton Kelly, whose patience and teaching skills opened new vistas and a workable insight into the pentatonic scale tradition, a vital link in the **JAZZ ANYONE . . . ?** system.

My first professional jazz job came in 1954 with an opportunity to perform and record with the Al Belletto Sextet on Capitol Records. Freddy Crane, pianist for the group, helped me discover that **LISTENING, IMITATING, and APPLYING** were the magic steps in **PLAYING** and **LEARNING** jazz music. Later, this group joined the Woody Herman Band for still deeper insights into big band jazz and what it takes to play it right!

The early '60's found me in Chicago and a member of the MJT+3 with Frank Strozier, Harold Mayburn, Bobby Cranshaw and Walter Perkins. Our recording called "Sleepy" hit the charts and we were on our way to New York. The maturity, originality and training of these seasoned players further developed my understanding and intuition of how this music is actually learned.

Playing night after night with Freddy Hubbard and George Coleman in the Slide Hampton Octet continued to reinforce the importance of understanding the jazz tradition, the harmonic system, cycles, patterns and chromatics that are the golden threads of the jazz language.

In 1967, I returned to Orlando to open the **BANDWAGON MUSIC CENTERS** with my life-long friend O.A. (Moe) Lowe. We played an integral part in helping develop jazz education interests and activities in area schools. By 1970, almost every Orlando area high school and many junior high schools had jazz programs scheduled in the curriculum. I became increasingly aware of the lack of suitable classroom jazz materials and began to put some ideas on paper.

In 1976, Valerie Dack, graciously collected my scribbled attempts and with her seasoned writing skills, began shaping a usable jazz curriculum – **JAZZ ANYONE . . . ?** was born! Rich Matteson, Matt Betton and other leading jazz educators recognized the unique qualities of our work and helped us spread the word. Soon, we were in our Micro-Mini Motor Home taking **JAZZ ANYONE . . . ?** to schools around the country.

The **JAZZ ANYONE . . . ?** story continues to unfold thanks to Dr. Sandy Feldstein, long-time friend and CPP/Belwin CEO, who has made it possible for me to research, write and publish the new **JAZZ ANYONE . . . ? PLAY AND LEARN SERIES.**

Hundreds of jazz players and teachers around the world have made important contributions to this work, among those not already mentioned are: Arch Martin, Bunky Green, Dick Dunscomb, Dr. William Lee, Dr. Warrick Carter, Bill McFarland, Jurgen Ohrem, Dr. Eric Maddox, Carl Fontana, Arnie Lawrence, Larry Riddley, Dr. Tom Ferguson, Jack Faas, Dr. Roger Cody, Dr. William Hinkle, Larry Green, Robert Foster, Dr. Ron McCurdy, Dr. William Prince, John Blair and Marion Scott.

In closing, I must give special thanks and recognition to my lifetime friend, Valerie, for giving so much of her life to this music. It was her personal support, wisdom, encouragement, tireless effort and most of all, her love that made **JAZZ ANYONE . . . ?** a living story for you to use in learning to play this wonderful American art form, jazz music.

Please enjoy,

Willie Thomas